Pupil Book 3

Spelling

Author: Chris Whitney

William Collins' dream of knowledge for all began with the publication of his first book in 1819. A self-educated mill worker, he not only enriched millions of lives, but also founded a flourishing publishing house. Today, staying true to this spirit, Collins books are packed with inspiration, innovation and practical expertise. They place you at the centre of a world of possibility and give you exactly what you need to explore it.

Collins. Freedom to teach.

Published by Collins
An imprint of HarperCollins*Publishers*
The News Building
1 London Bridge Street
London
SE1 9GF

Browse the complete Collins catalogue at
www.collins.co.uk

© HarperCollins*Publishers* Limited 2015

10 9 8 7 6 5 4 3 2 1

ISBN 978-0-00-813340-5

The author asserts her moral right to be identified as the author of this work.

British Library Cataloguing in Publication Data
A Catalogue record for this publication is available from the British Library

Edited by Jessica Marshall
Cover design and artwork by Amparo Barrera
Internal design concept by Amparo Barrera
Typesetting by Jouve
Illustrations by Beatriz Castro, Jacqui Davis, Eva Morales, Dante Ginevra, David Pavon, Aptara and QBS

Printed in Italy by Grafica Veneta S.p.A.

Pupil Book 3

Spelling

Contents

Adding suffixes beginning with vowels to words of more than one syllable

When you add a suffix starting with a vowel to a word of more than one syllable that ends in a vowel and a consonant, the spelling rule depends on whether the last syllable is stressed or not. If the last syllable is stressed, double the final consonant. For example: **gar**den + **er** = gardener, but be**gin** + **er** = begi**nn**er.

Get started

Copy and complete the chart by sorting these words into two groups. One has been done for you.

1. listened
2. listener
3. gardener
4. forgotten
5. watering
6. gardening
7. beginner
8. upsetting

Consonant not doubled	Consonant doubled
listened	

6

Try these

Copy and complete the sentences, then underline the misspelled word in each sentence. One has been done for you.

1. Janice <u>prefered</u> chocolate to ice-cream.

2. Ada had forgoten to buy a card for her mum.

3. Danu's teacher is transfering him from Class 1 to Class 2.

4. Kay was begining to enjoy tennis.

5. Ms Hardcastle presentted the school prizes.

Now try these

Copy and complete the sentences by choosing the correct spelling of each word. One has been done for you.

1. Max knew that he should not be <u>throwing</u> the grapes! (throwwing / throwing)

2. It was _____ for us to go into the forest by the school. (forbidden / forbiden)

3. Frida _____ carefully to the teacher's instructions. (listenned / listened)

4. Jo _____ not joining the cricket team at the start of term. (regreted / regretted)

5. Hanes enjoyed playing the flute, but he was only a _____. (beginner / begginner)

The i sound spelled y

In some words, the letter **y** is said as if it were an **i**. For example, the **y** in gym sounds like the **i** in rim. Here are some other words that follow this pattern:

- s**y**rup

- cr**y**stal

For these words, we spell the **i** sound with a letter **y**.

Get started

Copy the words, then underline the **i** sound spelled **y**. One has been done for you.

1. gym   *g**y**m*
2. myth
3. syrup
4. Egypt
5. crystal
6. pyramids
7. oxygen
8. typical

Try these

Copy and complete the sentences, then underline the words in which the **i** sound is spelled **y**. One has been done for you.

1. *I poured some <u>syrup</u> onto my porridge.*

2. My brother was pulling a funny face in the picture – it was typical of him!

3. Sal came up from underwater and took a big breath of oxygen.

4. The house with the yellow door was mysterious and old.

5. The glittering crystal glasses were on a silver tray.

6. Naveed's family is flying all the way to Egypt on holiday.

Now try these

Copy and complete the sentences by choosing the correct spelling of each word. One has been done for you.

1. *The doctor asked me about my <u>symptoms</u>.* (simptoms / symptoms)

2. The story was about a _____ beast with wings. (mythical / mithical)

3. Carin's jumper has the school _____ on it. (symbol / simbol)

4. Jeremy was always _____ in the shower! (singing / synging)

5. The distant land was ruled by a cruel _____. (king / kyng)

The u sound spelled ou

In some words, the letters **ou** are said as if they were a **u**. For example, the **ou** in touch sounds like the **u** in much. Some other words that follow this pattern are y**ou**ng and d**ou**ble.

Get started

Copy and complete the chart by sorting these words into two groups. One has been done for you.

1. young
2. cousin
3. count
4. mouth
5. noun
6. trouble
7. pound
8. double

Letters ou make the u sound	Letters ou do not make the u sound
young	

Try these

Copy and complete the sentences, then underline the words in which the letters **ou** make the **u** sound. One has been done for you.

1. My <u>younger</u> brother is out playing with his friends.

2. The new house is in the countryside.

3. Juan's cousin won an award – he was so proud of her!

4. There are a couple of clouds in the sky.

5. To score a point, just touch the ball to the ground.

6. If I do chores, I can double my two pounds pocket money.

Now try these

Copy and complete the sentences by choosing the correct spelling of each word. One has been done for you.

1. The married <u>couple</u> went on their honeymoon. (cuple / couple)

2. I was in a good mood, so I was _____ all the way to school. (humming / houmming)

3. Mr McCrury will _____ us if we're late! (punish / pounish)

4. Jeni hopes she has the _____ to sing on the stage. (currage / courage)

5. Patti fell and scraped her knee on the _____ step. (rugh / rough)

The prefixes dis- and mis-

The prefix **dis-** normally means **not**. For example:
dis- + agree = disagree.

The prefix **mis-** normally means **badly** or **incorrectly**.
For example: **mis- +spell = misspell**.

Sometimes we use the prefixes **dis-** and **mis-** when
there is not a clear root word.

Get started

Copy these words, then underline the prefixes. One has been done
for you.

1. disbelief   <u>dis</u>belief

2. mislead

3. disappear

4. mistreat

5. discomfort

6. misplace

7. disobey

8. misunderstand

Try these

Copy the words below, separating the prefix and root word.
One has been done for you.

1. misfortune   *mis / fortune*

2. disallow

3. disagreement

4. disadvantage

5. mishear

6. disobedient

Now try these

Copy and complete the sentences by choosing the correct
spelling of each word. One has been done for you.

1. *Dasu and Ben never <u>disagreed</u>
   on which game to play.*
   (disagreed / dis-agreed)

2. Finn was _____ with
   the football result.
   (dissappointed / disappointed)

3. Amelie _____ the
   question. (misheard / missheard)

4. Grace was _____ about how much
   chocolate she'd had. (dishonest / dis-honest)

5. He made the cards _____ in a puff of
   smoke! (dis-appear / disappear)

The prefixes in-, ir-, im- and il-

The prefix **in-** is used to mean 'not'. When you add **in-** to a root word, you do not change the spelling of the root word. But sometimes you do have to change the spelling of **in-**.

If you add **in-** to a root word beginning with **l**, **in-** becomes **il-**.

If you add **in-** to a root word beginning with **m** or **p**, **in-** becomes **im-**.

If you add **in-** to a root word beginning with **r**, **in-** becomes **ir-**.

Get started

Copy these words, then underline the prefixes. One has been done for you.

1. illegible
2. impossible
3. illegal
4. irresponsible
5. inactive
6. impatient
7. intolerant
8. immobile

 illegible

Try these

Copy these root words, then add the prefixes **in-**, **ir-**, **im-** or **il-**.
One has been done for you.

1. convenient   *inconvenient*

2. correct

3. capable

4. literate

5. responsible

6. competent

7. proper

Now try these

Copy and complete the sentences by choosing the correct
spelling for each word. One has been done for you.

1. *Akhil's skiing holiday was
<u>incredible</u>.* (incredible / imcredible)

2. Antonia found the chocolate cake
_____! (imresistable / irresistible)

3. Christopher's handwriting was
_____. (illegible / inlegible)

4. My brother can be so childish and
_____. (inmature / immature)

5. I got five _____ answers in my maths test.
(incorrect / uncorrect)

The prefixes re- and inter-

Prefixes change the meaning of the root word. The prefix **re-** means **again**. The prefix **inter-** means **between** or **among**. When you add **re-** or **inter-** to a word, you do not have to make any changes to the root word.

Get started

Copy the words and then underline the prefix in each word. One has been done for you.

1. interview   *interview*

2. rename
3. rewrite
4. redo
5. interlude
6. interrupt
7. interaction
8. react

Try these

Copy the words, then add the prefix **re-** or **inter-**. One has been done for you.

1. value   *revalue*
2. play
3. national
4. assemble
5. dial
6. claim
7. join
8. deliver

Now try these

Copy and complete the sentences by adding the correct prefix. One has been done for you.

1. *It was busy at Exeter International Airport today.*
2. Mo waited for the rainbow to _____appear.
3. I need to do lots of _____vision for my exams.
4. It was a long, slow _____city bus journey.
5. Today I am going to _____organise my desk.
6. The Johnsons want to _____locate to a new area.

The prefixes sub- and super-

A prefix is a group of letters that you can add to the start of a root word. The prefix **sub-** means **under** or **less than**. The prefix **super-** means **above** or **more than**. When you add **sub-** or **super-** to a root word, you do not change the spelling of the root word.

Get started

Copy these words and underline the prefixes in each word. One has been done for you.

1. supermarket

   supermarket

2. submarine

3. superstar

4. subway

5. superhuman

6. superstore

7. subtract

8. subscribe

Try these

Copy the root words then add the prefix **sub-** or **super-**. One has been done for you.

1. title   _subtitle_
2. heading
3. market
4. section
5. size
6. man
7. vision
8. merge

Now try these

Copy and complete the sentences by writing the missing prefix. One has been done for you.

1. _The new <u>super</u>market opened last week._
2. The atmosphere at the match was _____dued.
3. He lifted the car with _____human strength.
4. Never use sharp knives without _____vision.
5. Jael cancelled her _____scription to the magazine.
6. The _____mariners lived aboard their _____marine.

The prefixes anti- and auto-

A prefix is a group of letters added to the start of a root word. The prefix **anti-** is used to mean **against**. The prefix **auto-** is used to mean **self** or **own**.

Get started

Copy these words then underline the prefixes. One has been done for you.

1. automatic   <u>auto</u>matic
2. anticlockwise
3. antiseptic
4. automobile
5. antisocial
6. antibiotics

Try these

Copy the root words then add the prefix **anti-** or **auto-**. One has been done for you.

1. graph   *autograph*
2. climax
3. pilot
4. freeze
5. hero
6. clockwise

Now try these

Copy and complete the sentences by writing the missing prefixes. One has been done for you.

1. *For some spider bites there is no <u>anti</u>dote.*
2. The band signed ____graphs as they left the concert.
3. Littering and drawing graffiti are ____social activities.
4. What a life she has led! She should write an ____biography.
5. I cleaned his cuts and grazes with ____bacterial wipes.
6. The end of the film was a disappointing ____climax.

The suffix -ation

A suffix is a group of letters added to the end of a root word. The suffix **-ation** turns verbs into nouns. If the verb ends in an **e**, remove the **e** before adding **-ation**.

Get started

Copy and complete the chart by sorting the words into two groups. One has been done for you.

1. formation
2. continuation
3. sensation
4. continueation
5. senseation
6. admireation
7. determineation
8. admiration

Correctly spelled words	Incorrectly spelled words
formation	

Try these

Copy these verbs and turn them into nouns by adding **-ation**. One has been done for you.

1. limit   *limitation*

2. inspire

3. explore

4. observe

5. compile

6. reserve

Now try these

Copy and complete the sentences by adding **-ation** to one verb in each sentence. One has been done for you.

1. The children read the inform on the poster.

Answer: *The children read the* <u>*information*</u> *on the poster.*

2. Rahul was full of admire for his hero.

3. Carl made a reserve at the restaurant.

4. Anika makes observe of rare birds.

5. We should support the conserve of wildlife.

6. Oscar studied hard in prepare for his exams.

Adding the suffix -ly to words ending with y

If you add the suffix **-ly** to an adjective, you can turn it into an adverb. Normally, you can add **-ly** to a root word without changing the spelling. However, if the root word ends with **y** and is longer than one syllable, you must change the final **y** into an **i** before you add **-ly**.

Get started

Copy these words, then underline the suffix **-ly**. One has been done for you.

1. sleepily   *sleep<u>ily</u>*
2. prettily
3. breezily
4. cheekily
5. messily
6. shakily
7. angrily
8. hungrily

Try these

Copy the root words, then add the suffix **-ly**. One has been done for you.

1. nasty   *nastily*
2. hasty
3. ready
4. grumpy
5. busy
6. easy

Now try these

Copy and complete these sentences by choosing the correct spelling. One has been done for you.

1. *The man tucked into the hamburger* *hungrily*. (hungrily / hungryly)
2. The visitor was dressed_____.
   (shabbily / shabbly)
3. The boy wrote _____ on the form. (shakly / shakily)
4. The man walked to his car_____.
   (happily / happyly)
5. The thief left the building _____. (hastily / hastly)
6. The racing car zoomed _____ around the corner. (noisely / noisily)

The pattern -sure as in measure

The **sher** sound at the end of words is spelled **sure**.

Get started

Say the words below aloud and listen to the **sure** pattern. Copy them and underline the letters that make the pattern. The first one has been done for you.

1. treasure
2. leisure
3. assure
4. pleasure
5. enclosure
6. measure
7. reassure
8. insure

trea<u>sure</u>

Try these

Correct the spelling errors in each word. One has been done for you.

1. compozure   *composure*
2. displeashure
3. expozure
4. leishure
5. clozure
6. disclosuer

Now try these

Use the words below in sentences of your own. One has been done for you.

1. *Bess fed the puppies in the <u>enclosure</u>.* (locsunree)
2. measure
3. treasure
4. displeasure
5. leisure
6. pleasure

The endings -ture and -cher

Words that end with a **cher** sound often have the letter pattern **-ture**.

But do remember: some words are spelled exactly as they sound. For example: ri**cher** and cat**cher**

Get started

Copy the words then underline the **cher** sound. One has been done for you.

1. furniture   *furni<u>ture</u>*
2. capture
3. vulture
4. creature
5. nature
6. adventure
7. puncture
8. rupture

Try these

Correct the spelling mistakes in the list below. One has been done for you.

1. piccher

   Answer: *picture*

2. moistcher

3. tempercher

4. futuer

5. fractcher

6. postior

Now try these

Use the words below in sentences of your own. One has been done for you.

1. *Bears are woodland <u>creatures</u>.*

2. nature

3. capture

4. picture

5. adventure

6. pastures

The ending -sion

The **shun** sound at the end of words can often be spelt -**sion**.

Get started

Copy the words and underline the **shun** sound. One has been done for you.

1. television

Answer: *television*

2. division

3. vision

4. confusion

5. invasion

6. decision

7. mansion

8. extension

Try these

Choose the correct spelling for each word. One has been done for you.

1. illusion / illusion   *illusion*
2. revision / revission
3. conclusion / conclution
4. occasion / occastion
5. collission / collision
6. version / vershun

Now try these

Use the words below in sentences of your own. One has been done for you.

1. confusion

   Answer: *There was <u>confusion</u> over school opening times.*

2. division
3. illusion
4. conclusion
5. revision
6. collision
7. invasion

The suffix -ous

Many adjectives end with the suffix **-ous**.

Add the suffix **-ous** to the end of the root word.

If the root word ends with **e**, like **fame**, you normally drop the **e** before adding **-ous**.

If the root word ends with a soft **g** sound, you keep the final **e**.

If the root word ends with **y**, like **vary**, you change **y** to **i** before adding **-ous**.

If the root word ends with **-our,** you change **-our** to **-or** before adding the **-ous**.

Sometimes there is not a clear root word.

If there is an **ee** sound before the **-ous,** it is normally spelled with an **i**. However, sometimes this **ee** sound is spelled with an **e**.

Get started

Copy the words and underline the suffix **-ous**. One has been done for you.

1. ravenous   *ravenous*
2. poisonous
3. fabulous
4. nervous
5. ridiculous
6. hazardous

Try these

Copy the words then add the **-ous** ending. You may need to remove letters too. One has been done for you.

1. vary   *various*
2. courage
3. humour
4. advantage
5. prosper
6. fame
7. adventure

Now try these

Use the words below in sentences of your own. One has been done for you.

1. curious

   Answer: *Cats have a reputation for being <u>curious</u>.*

2. dangerous
3. glamorous
4. mountainous

5. hideous
6. nervous

The endings -tion, -sion, -ssion and -cian

There are different ways of spelling the **shun** sound: **-tion**, **-ssion**, **-sion** and **-cian**.

The most common way of spelling the **shun** sound is **-tion**. Use this when the root word ends in **t** or **te**.

For root words ending in **-ss** or **-mit**, spell the **shun** sound **-ssion**.

If the root word ends in **te**, like **complete**, drop the final **e** before adding **-ion**.

For root words ending in **d** or a consonant then **se**, spell the **shun** sound **-sion**. If the root word ends in **d**, like **extend**, drop the **d** before adding **-sion**.

For root words ending in **c** or **cs**, spell the **shun** sound **-cian**. If the root word ends in **cs**, drop the final **s** before adding **-ian**.

Get started

Copy the words then underline the different ways of spelling the **shun** sound. One has been done for you.

1. discussion

   Answer: _discussion_

2. action

3. tension

4. musician

5. admission

6. percussion

7. election

Try these

Choose the correct spelling of the **shun** sound for each word.
One has been done for you.

1. invenssion / invension / invention

   Answer: *invention*

2. politission / politician / politision

3. injection / injecssion / injecsion

4. magition / magission / magician

5. eruption / erupcian / erupsion

6. perfeccian / perfection / perfecsion

Now try these

Copy and complete the sentences by adding the correct suffix
to the underlined words. One has been done for you.

1. *Rover the dog knew the direction home.*

2. The <u>May</u>or worried about the coming <u>elect</u>.

3. My sister is a very talented <u>music</u>.

4. I can recite the alphabet without <u>hesitate</u>.

5. Football is Cynthia's growing <u>obsess</u>.

6. It is important to get a good <u>educate</u>.

The k sound spelled ch

There are several ways of spelling the **k** sound. In some words the **k** sound is spelled **ch**.

For example:

- a**ch**e
- **ch**aracter

Get started

Copy these words and underline the letters that make the **k** sound. One has been done for you.

1. headache   *heada<u>ch</u>e*
2. chemist
3. chorus
4. scheme
5. stomach
6. school
7. chord
8. mechanic

Try these

Copy the sentences then underline the words in which the **k** sound is spelled **ch**. One has been done for you.

1. Tom's <u>stomach</u> hurt from eating too much cheese.

2. Cherries always give me tummy ache.

3. Charles called out and his voice made an echo.

4. The school rabbit was munching a carrot.

5. The room was in chaos, but Gran still looked cheery.

Now try these

Copy and complete the sentences by choosing the correct spelling of the words. One has been done for you.

1. *Nina was looking forward to the* <u>*school*</u> *disco.* (skool / school)

2. We went to the _____ with my aunt. (market / marchet)

3. Flavia plays the saxophone in our town _____. (orchestra / orkestra)

4. The _____ old lady had made a cake. (chind / kind)

5. We made the _____ such a mess! (kitchen / chitchen)

The sh sound spelled ch

In most words, the **sh** sound is spelled as it is said, with the letters **sh** as in **sh**ower.

However, in some words the **sh** sound is spelled with the letters **ch** as in **ch**ef.

Get started

Copy and complete the chart by sorting these words into two groups. One has been done for you.

1. moustache
2. chef
3. ship
4. machine
5. fashion
6. chalet
7. brochure
8. dish

sh sound spelled ch	sh sound spelled sh
moustache	

Try these

Copy and complete the words by using the letters **ch** or **sh**.
One has been done for you.

1. _ _andelier

   Answer: _chandelier_

2. ca_ _ ier

3. qui_ _e

4. a_ _amed

5. sa_ _et

6. cu_ _ion

Now try these

Copy and complete the sentences by choosing the correct
spelling. One has been done for you.

1. _The parachutist floated safely
   to the ground._
   (parachutist / parashutist)

2. I don't really care about following
   _____. (fachion / fashion)

3. The meal was cooked by an
   excellent _____. (chef / shef)

4. I like a _____ topping on my pizza.
   (muchroom / mushroom)

5. I have a _____ every day. (chower / shower)

The sound k spelled -que and the sound g spelled -gue

In some words, the **k** sound is spelled **-que**. In some words, the **g** sound is spelled **-gue**.

Get started

Copy and complete the chart by sorting these words into two groups. One has been done for you.

1. arabesque
2. antique
3. cheque
4. tongue
5. rogue
6. league
7. boutique
8. meringue

-que	-gue
arabesque	

Try these

Copy and complete the root words by adding **que** or **gue**. One has been done for you.

1. ton_ _ _

   Answer: *tongue*

2. lea _ _ _

3. anti _ _ _

4. ro _ _ _

5. bouti _ _ _

Now try these

Copy and complete the sentences by choosing the correct spelling. One has been done for you.

1. *The film about sharks contained very little <u>dialogue</u>.*
   (dialogue / dialoque)

2. The Normans _____ England in 1066. (conguered / conquered)

3. The millionaire signed a large _____. (chegue / cheque)

4. The Great _____ was also known as the Black Death. (Plague / Plaque)

5. We had to _____ for ages at the supermarket. (gueue / queue)

The sound s spelled sc

There are different ways of spelling the **s** sound. One way to spell it is with **sc.**

Get started

Copy and complete the chart by sorting these words into two groups. One has been done for you.

1. song
2. descend
3. decent
4. scene
5. seen
6. scent
7. sent
8. crescent

s spelled sc	s spelled s or c
	song

Try these

Copy the words and underline **sc** in each word. One has been done for you.

1. scissors

Answer: <u>sc</u>issors

2. descend

3. abscess

4. scent

5. scenery

6. fascinate

Now try these

Use the words below in sentences of your own. You may use a dictionary if you need to. The first one has been done for you.

1. scenic

Answer: *Helen and Andrew walked a <u>sc</u>enic route.*

2. muscles

3. crescent

4. scent

5. Science

The sound ay spelled ei, eigh and ey

There are lots of different ways of spelling the **ay** sound. Three ways to spell the sound **ay** are with the letters **ei**, **eigh** or **ey**.

Get started

Copy and complete the chart by sorting these words into three groups. One has been done for you.

1. beige
2. eighteen
3. weightlifter
4. convey
5. neighbourhood
6. paperweight
7. survey
8. prey

ay spelled ei	ay spelled eigh	ay spelled ey
beige		

Try these

Copy these words then underline the letters that are used for the **ay** sound in each word. One has been done for you.

1. eight   <u>eight</u>

2. obey

3. sleigh

4. veil

5. eighty

Now try these

Copy and complete the sentences by choosing the correct spelling. One has been done for you.

1. The tiger stalks its <u>prey</u>.
   (prei / preigh / prey)

2. Hamid's alarm clock rang at
   _____ o'clock. (eit / eight / eyt)

3. The old man had a _____ beard.
   (grei / greigh / grey)

4. The King's _____ lasted many
   years. (rein / reighn / reyn)

5. Blood runs through our _____.
   (veins / veighns / veyns)

45

The possessive apostrophe with plural words

To show that something belongs to more than one person or thing, use a possessive apostrophe. Put this after the plural form of the word.

Some plural words don't end in **s**. For these words, add an **s** after the apostrophe.

Some singular nouns already end in an **s**. For these words, add another **s** after the apostrophe.

Get started

Copy the two columns of words and then match each singular word with its plural. One has been done for you.

1. *girl*   **a)** puppies

2. cat   **b)** men

3. child   **c)** geese

4. lorry   **d)** cats

5. puppy   **e)** lorries

6. chair   **f)** *girls*

7. man   **g)** children

8. goose   **h)** chairs

Try these

Copy each sentence and decide whether the underlined word is singular or plural. One has been done for you.

1. *The <u>puppies'</u> toys were chewed.*   *plural*
2. The <u>goose's</u> egg was golden.
3. The <u>cat's</u> food was in the bowl.
4. The <u>men's</u> coats were warm.
5. The <u>girls'</u> hair bands were white.

Now try these

Copy and complete the sentences with the correct use of the possessive apostrophe. One has been done for you.

1. *Chloe held on tightly to the <u>puppies'</u> leads.*
   (puppy's / puppies')

2. The _____ covers were worn.
   (books' / book's)

3. The _____ boots were
   waterproof. (women's / womens's)

4. _____favourite drink was
   milkshake. (James's / Jame's)

5. Khalid stayed at his_____ house.
   (friends' / friend's)

47

Homophones and near-homophones (I)

Homophones are words that sound the same but they are spelled differently and have different meanings.

Get started

Put the words into homophone pairs. One has been done for you.

bury	accept	medal	except	who's	effect
berry	meddle	affect	weather	whether	whose

Answer: *berry, bury*

Copy and complete the definitions with words from the list. One has been done for you.

1. <u>*berry*</u>: a small juicy fruit that does not have a stone

2. _____: a contraction of the words **who** and **is** or **has**

3. _____: belonging to

4. _____: to interfere or tinker

5. _____: not including

6. _____: put in a hole and cover with earth

Try these

Copy the list of words and add the homphones. One has been done for you.

1. medal

   Answer: *meddle*

2. except

3. who's

4. effect

5. bury

Now try these

Copy and complete the sentences by choosing the correct homophone. One has been done for you.

1. *The <u>weather</u> was good for the school trip.* (whether / weather)

2. Samira _____ the party invitation. (accepted / excepted)

3. Squirrels love to _____ nuts in the garden. (bury / berry)

4. Jack proudly showed off his swimming _____. (medal / meddle)

5. I bought a cake with a _____ on top. (bury / berry)

Homophones and near-homophones (2)

Homophones are words that sound the same but they are spelled differently and have different meanings.

Get started

Put the words into homophone pairs. One has been done for you.

hear	grate	grown	here	great
heal	knot	heel	groan	not

Answer: *heal, heel*

Copy and complete the definitions with words from the list. One has been done for you.

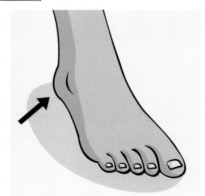

1. <u>heel</u>: *the back part of the foot*

2. _____: a contraction of the words **he** and **will**

3. _____: to become healthy again

4. _____: when something has become larger

5. _____: a noise of pain or despair

Try these

Copy the list of words and add the homophones. One has been done for you.

1. great

   Answer: *grate*

2. grown

3. heel

4. knot

5. hear

Now try these

Copy and complete the sentences by choosing the correct homophone. One has been done for you.

1. *Dogs can <u>hear</u> very high pitched sounds.* (hear / here)

2. Tessa let out a _____ at the awful joke. (groan / grown)

3. The sailor was glad he could tie so many_____. (knots / nots)

4. The cut on Majid's finger would not _____. (heel / he'll / heal)

5. The new shoes hurt Sheila's _____. (heal / he'll / heel)

Homophones and near-homophones (3)

Homophones are words that sound the same but they are spelled differently and have different meanings.

Get started

Put the words into homophone pairs.
One has been done for you.

mist	plane	fair	missed
mane	peace	meat	plain
main	meet	fare	piece

Answer: *meet, meat*

Copy and complete the definitions with words from the list.
One has been done for you.

1. <u>mane</u>: *long hair on the neck of a horse or lion*

2. _____ : a wide, flat, level surface

3. _____ : simple, basic or without decoration

4. _____ : tiny drops of water in the air

5. _____ : a part of something

6. _____ : the amount you pay to travel on a train

7. _____ : the flesh of animals

8. _____ : a state of calm or quiet

Try these

Copy the misspelled words in each set. Some have more than one. One has been done for you.

1. plain   plaine   plane

Answer: *plaine*

2. peace   peece   peaze

3. missed   myst   mist

4. meit   miet   meet

5. peese   piece   peice

6. fare   fair   fayer

Now try these

Copy and complete the sentences by choosing the correct spelling of the words. One has been done for you.

1. *The horse's <u>mane</u> was brushed for the show.* (main / mane)

2. The damp _____ rose from the river. (missed / mist)

3. The wind swept across the grassy _____. (plain / plane)

4. Jamil found the last _____ of the jigsaw. (peace / piece)

5. I went on all the scary rides at the _____. (fair / fare)

53

Homophones and near-homophones (4)

Homophones are words that sound the same but they are spelled differently and have different meanings.

Get started

Put the words into homophone pairs. One has been done for you.

| ball | brake | male | break | mail | rain | scene | seen | bawl | rein |

Answer: *mail, male*

Copy and complete the definitions with words from the list. One has been done for you.

1. <u>*mail*</u>: *letters and parcels*

2. _____: water falling from the sky

3. _____: a strap for guiding horses

4. _____: to cry loudly

Try these

Copy the list of words and add the homophones. One has been done for you.

1. rain

   Answer: *rein*

2. ball

3. seen

4. scene

5. break

Now try these

Copy and complete the sentences by choosing the correct spelling of the words. One has been done for you.

1. *Tariq was determined to <u>break</u> all his racing records.* (brake / break)

2. A _____ sheep is called a ram. (mail / male)

3. It was the biggest cake I had ever _____. (scene / seen)

4. The _____ were made of leather. (rains / reigns / reins)

5. To stop the car, press down on the _____. (brake / break)